Vincent Iduh

Simulation model for public transport traffic flow using GPS data

Vincent Idah

Simulation model for public transport traffic flow using GPS data

LAP LAMBERT Academic Publishing

Impressum / Imprint

Bibliografische Information der Deutschen Nationalbibliothek: Die Deutsche Nationalbibliothek verzeichnet diese Publikation in der Deutschen Nationalbibliografie; detaillierte bibliografische Daten sind im Internet über http://dnb.d-nb.de abrufbar.
Alle in diesem Buch genannten Marken und Produktnamen unterliegen warenzeichen-, marken- oder patentrechtlichem Schutz bzw. sind Warenzeichen oder eingetragene Warenzeichen der jeweiligen Inhaber. Die Wiedergabe von Marken, Produktnamen, Gebrauchsnamen, Handelsnamen, Warenbezeichnungen u.s.w. in diesem Werk berechtigt auch ohne besondere Kennzeichnung nicht zu der Annahme, dass solche Namen im Sinne der Warenzeichen- und Markenschutzgesetzgebung als frei zu betrachten wären und daher von jedermann benutzt werden dürften.

Bibliographic information published by the Deutsche Nationalbibliothek: The Deutsche Nationalbibliothek lists this publication in the Deutsche Nationalbibliografie; detailed bibliographic data are available in the Internet at http://dnb.d-nb.de.
Any brand names and product names mentioned in this book are subject to trademark, brand or patent protection and are trademarks or registered trademarks of their respective holders. The use of brand names, product names, common names, trade names, product descriptions etc. even without a particular marking in this works is in no way to be construed to mean that such names may be regarded as unrestricted in respect of trademark and brand protection legislation and could thus be used by anyone.

Coverbild / Cover image: www.ingimage.com

Verlag / Publisher:
LAP LAMBERT Academic Publishing
ist ein Imprint der / is a trademark of
OmniScriptum GmbH & Co. KG
Heinrich-Böcking-Str. 6-8, 66121 Saarbrücken, Deutschland / Germany
Email: info@lap-publishing.com

Herstellung: siehe letzte Seite /
Printed at: see last page
ISBN: 978-3-659-62871-9

Zugl. / Approved by: Nairobi,University of Nairobi,Diss.,2014

Acknowledgment

To the Almighty for this great gift of life so as to accomplish this far I have come.

To my loved ones, for their great support and encouragement throughout my academic years.

To my supervisor Prof Peter Wagacha who has opened my eyes to the research world. His guidance, support, and positive criticism made this project a success. To the panellists, Dr. Elisha Opiyo to whom I am grateful for positive criticism that has led to success of this project.

To my classmates and friends, who shared ideas and provided assistance during this project, I say Thank You!

Table of Contents

List of Figures

List of Tables

Abbreviations

GTFS- General Transit Feed Specification

GSM- Global System for Mobile

LCD- Liquid Crystal Display

ATIS- Advanced Traveller Information System

GPS- Global positioning System

CCTV- Closed Circuit Television

CHAPTER ONE

INTRODUCTION

1.1   Background of Study

System management is that makes it easier for the running of activities and therefore provides reliable and efficient information which will be used in decision making improvement. The system is used to integrate collected data from inputs to provide information that is necessary by users who require it. This provides efficiency in the storage, retrieval and updating of data to users requirements.

Traffic is the number of vehicles passing a given point in a given time.

Traffic congestion is the condition on road networks that occurs when use increases, and is characterized by slower speeds, longer trip times, and increased vehicular queuing.

Traffic flow is the interactions between vehicles, drivers and infrastructure, with the aim of understanding and developing a road network with efficient movement of traffic and minimal traffic congestion problems. The total number of vehicles passing a given point in a given time.

Modeling transit systems is an integral part of travel demand modeling. To accomplish this task, modeling agencies go through the tedious process of coding the entire transit network and update it periodically to reflect the changes in service characteristics.GTFS a platform started by Google is now seen to be used by many modeling agencies, as a means to publish their service characteristics.GTFS data is important for travel modeling, essentially for accessibility measures in terms of mapping various routes. It is also used by third-party software applications in providing real time information, visualization, trip planning, mobile data, and interactive voice response (IVR) systems.

According to Cambridge, transportation system in Sub-Saharan Africa is not designed to accommodate current number of rod vehicles, let alone future growth. Transit system for the public is not robust enough to help ease demand. Traffic congestion is bad impeding economic development, increased inequality as people outside the city struggle to commute to work.

Traffic congestion issues include:

- Rapid urbanization

10

- High rate of Motorization
- Lack of infrastructure, enforcement, management and regulation.

Other issues of traffic congestion will consist of road safety due to traffic deaths, more vehicles crammed onto the roads, air pollution. Pollution has been a major part among the issues that come with traffic congestion, in that the old models people import from Europe has been seen not to have met emission standards in those countries. Emissions from these vehicles also contribute to global warming and this causes climate change which further brings forth floods or drought leading to reduced agricultural production. This reduction of agriculture production worsens food security which leads to spread of disease later causing increase risk of conflict over scarce land and resources. The question that is quite evident is that of is it more roads or cars needed or better policy to be implemented.

Traffic congestion in South Africa Johannesburg has been rated more than that of New York City this is followed by the likes of Moscow, Istanbul, and Warsaw respectively. In East Africa (Sustran) Sustainable Transport in East Africa cities was initiated aimed at reducing growth in private motorized vehicles, thus reducing traffic congestion and green house gas emissions.

This initiative tends to initiate the upgrading of public transport systems, implement improved non-motorized transport infrastructure (bicycle and walkways), and apply travel demand management eg. Parking reforms and other supporting policies.

The sole purpose for traffic flow management to avoid congestion is to get drivers and passengers to their destinations faster, safer and greener. Drivers should have exact route information and arrival times by building a precise view of traffic flow over entire road network.

This system will have the model of the road network used by public service vehicles and their various routes. This information will be helpful for traffic flow management. Alternate routes will be easier to locate, since the view of your current position and other adjacent routes is available.

1.2   Problem Statement

The road network in Nakuru Town is quite squeezed in that the roads accessing it are small, to be able to cater for the increased number of motorists. There are no designated pathways for cyclists and motorbikes who also use the roads just as their counterparts with vehicles, this leading to the increased congestion. Mass transit and non-motorized transport was not considered in making of the roads in this town thus traffic flow being made slow, leading to poor economic growth. People are not able to access various amenities, since they identify places with buildings rather than roads leading to them. Traffic congestion in this town is only at two points which are at Railways Flyover entering town, and Mburu Gichua roundabout into town from LangaLanga.

1.3 Objectives

- To create GTFS data for Nakuru Town road network.
- To use GTFS data to model public transport routes around the town.
- To be able to simulate traffic flow using vehicle speeds.

1.4 Justification

Transport is a driver of development, and when integrated and efficient transport system is designed correctly leads to prosperity by providing access to water, food, and education. Importance of efficient, low cost mass transit and non-motorized transport is a means of helping to alleviate poverty, spurring economy in urban centres, and providing alternative and affordable transport.

Transport flow management is needed as set of strategic practices utilized by those in authority, to ensure uniform vehicle flow and avoid delays due to congestion and ultimately improving safety. This system is to be able to help predict traffic congestion through known traffic flow and thus be able to avoid congestion in future.

1.5 Scope and Limitations

(1) The system will be for depicting traffic congestion of Nakuru Town.

(2) The study will be specifically for public service vehicles excluding private vehicles.

(3) Time intervals to be used to locate traffic congestion areas will be those of peak hours (morning and evening) only.

CHAPTER TWO

LITERATURE REVIEW

2.1 Introduction

The sole purpose of this chapter is to really analyze, identify what others have done in your area of interest, and make conclusions based on the research. Literature review uses as its database reports of primary or original scholarship, and does not report new primary scholarship itself. The primary reports used in the literature may be verbal, but in the vast majority of cases reports are written documents. The types of scholarships may be empirical, theoretical, critical/analytical, or methodological in nature (Cooper 1988).

In order to develop a project to its success, the current systems are identified, reviewed and analyzed. These systems have been categorized as either automation systems or management software.

(Horn, 2013) presented a new algorithm for alleviating traffic flow instabilities, which could be implemented by a variation of the adaptive cruise-control systems that are an option on many of current vehicles. He does this using a car with an adaptive cruise control using sensors, such as radar or laser rangefinders, to monitor the speed and distance of the car in front of it. That way, the driver does not have to turn the cruise control off when there is traffic congestion. The car will automatically slow when it needs to and return to its programmed speed when possible. He reiterates that, a car equipped with the said system would also use sensor information about the distance and velocity of the car behind it, thus referring to the system to having bilateral control. Instabilities arise, because variations in velocity are magnified as they pass through a lane of traffic.

(Priyadarshana et al., 2013) mentions that both government and non-government parties have taken many actions to reduce this problem but it remains as it was. Solutions to this problem of traffic congestion include DialogSatNav, Mobitel T-Navi. SatNav system provides automated and voice supported navigation with the use of GPS data. It is implemented with a detailed map of Sri Lanka, which enables to assist navigating to and from any destination in Sri Lanka. Another GPS system system called T-Navi partners with Mobitel to provide live updates on traffic jams or road congestion. This system consists of 3D moving map and guidance components. Map displays static as well as dynamic places of interest. It offers turn-by-turn direction to users and also direct users to destination through routes based on traffic condition.

Similarly according to (Aslam, et al., 2012) presented a congestion-aware route planning system. In this they learned the congestion model based on real data from a fleet of taxis and loop detectors. Using this learned street-level congestion model, they developed a congestion-aware traffic planning system that operates in one of two modes: (1) to achieve the social optimum path with respect to travel time over all the drivers in the system or (2) to optimize individual travel times. They evaluated the performance of this system using 10,000+ taxis trips and showed that on average their approach improved the total travel time by 15%. The main contributions were:

- The first study estimating the flow-delay function at city scale using sensor data from road-side loop detectors and a roving fleet of taxis.
- A traffic routing system that uses the flow-delay function to estimate street-level congestion models and implements multi-user congestion-aware routing with the social optimum guarantee.
- An experimental comparison between actual taxi paths, socially optimal congestion-aware routing greedy path planning.

(Benhamza et al., 2012). Agent based modelling aims to develop a unique traffic simulation system that can be used to study traffic theory and assess network infrastructure and control changes. Its main objectives include gaining an understanding of traffic theory, learning the major features and issues of traffic simulation, and evaluating agent-based modelling as a means of simulating traffic.

(Marfia et al., 2012) expresses that vehicular congestion in urban areas has steadily grown during the years to become one of the primary problems tackled by city administrators. The increase of wasted time and pollution due to vehicular traffic has paved the way to many different countermeasures, ranging from the enforcement of congestion tolls to the commercialization of vehicles powered by low-emission hybrid engines. Advanced traveler information systems (ATISs) which are capable of supplying updated traffic information to all those citizens that are driving through city roads, represent a prominent approach to combat vehicular congestion. ATISs are concerned with collecting, processing, and disseminating traffic information, providing data that can be profitably exploited by an on-board navigation system to compute the most convenient route to a given destination. Indeed,

14

their role becomes progressively more relevant as their accuracy and reliability increases, thus encouraging more and more people to utilize them while driving. With this they devised a new congestion detection model that accurately estimates and forecasts the short-term congestion state of a road without requiring any prior knowledge regarding any of its parameters. Such a model can be easily integrated within an ATIS and usefully applied to a given road.

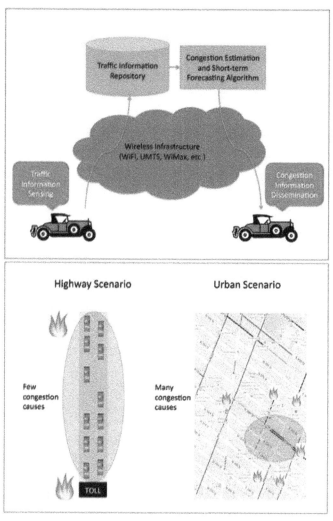

Figure 1: Congestion Prediction Model

15

(Pereira, 2011) comprehends the final road towards the coupling of both a traffic simulator and a robotics simulator, SUMO and USARSim respectively. Having addressed all particular issues in each simulator, a comprehensive analysis to their integration is performed, with focus on the practical usability of the platform and encountered difficulties. A simple reactive agent was also modeled and implemented to validate the platform. It consists of simple GUI showing information relative to vehicle sensors, and an automatic control. SUMO calculates the surrounding vehicles around an autonomous vehicle. Therefore, a control code to handle creation, moving and deletion of the former is presented. It uses a hash-table comprehending vehicles already created on the scene, and calculates their next movements. Its pseudo code in algorithm AbsMove(veh), Create(veh) and Kill(veh) correspond to the WorldController USARSim commands. Having imported the road network into SUMO using the netEditor and to USARSim using the procedural modeling application, they implemented the traffic network coherence and calibration method between simulators. As both networks for the two simulators rely on different sources, albeit they both resemble the same physical zone in question. Moreover, to solve this issue a coordinate transformation method is used and presented which should be feasible to transform each point on SUMO system coordinate to USARSim and vice-versa.

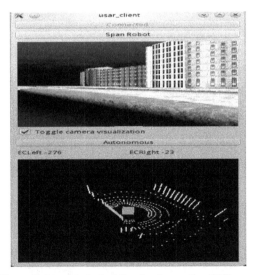

Figure 2: A screenshot of the simple reactive GUI agent

(Bajpai, 2011) shares an adaptive control algorithm as an important strategy to manage traffic at an intersection. These are improvements of vehicle actuated signal control, where explicitly strategies are formulated to compute the signal timing considering the current traffic state obtained from sensors.

However, field evaluation of these strategies is cumbersome and expensive and hence simulators which model traffic system can be a good alternative. The main challenge was a good interface between the signal control system and the traffic simulators. The signal control system needed the state of the junction in terms of vehicle occupancy at every instant. On the other hand, traffic simulator needs information on whether the signal state has changed. This two way communication required an efficient interface which is similar to client-server architecture. The simulator acted as the server where as the adaptive control strategy act like client. He proposed an efficient interface to couple adaptive control strategy and traffic simulator. This interface mediates between traffic control system and traffic simulator and provides online interaction to simulation from the control strategy. This interface facilitates pure procedural routines to communicate and is written in C language along with Python/C API. Additionally, a module to estimate the vehicular delay due to the control strategy is developed. This delay is estimated by defining effective length of queue, which is provided as a user input. This interface is tested using SUMO (Simulation for Urban Mobility). The traffic control strategy is analogous to the HCM vehicle actuated traffic control except that there is a queue prediction model which computes upper limits on the maximum green time. An isolated four arm junction having four phases is simulated for various flow conditions. The simulator supplied the state of the downstream detector to the traffic control algorithm at every simulation step and the control algorithm determines the signal time strategies (phase termination, green extension, and maximum green time). These strategies communicated to the simulator. These communications were facilitated by the proposed interface. The average stopped delay was computed as the performance parameter. The interface was also coupled with another traffic simulator (VISSIM) and the results compared. This interface justified the concept of reusability by the evaluation of number of control strategy.

.

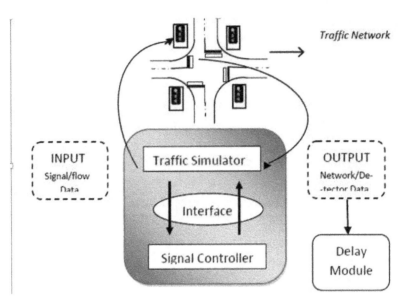

Figure 3:Architecture of the interface which couples signal controller and traffic simulator.

(Dobler, 2011), tries to compare and contrast macro-simulation with micro-simulation. He sees macro-simulation as one based on aggregated data, flows instead of individual movement, often planning networks. Additionally, he views micro-simulation in that population is modeled as a set of individuals. Traffic flows are based on the movement of single vehicles (or agents) and their interactions. Also various traffic flow models are included for instance, cellular automata model, queue model or car following model.Oftenly, high resolution networks for instance navigation quality is also inclusive.

2.2 Traffic Congestion Alert Systems

Many automation systems have been developed but in one way or another few have found way in the Kenyan market. There are some factors that hinder their operation in Kenya, and this include

1. The lack of receivers and transmitters on the junctions of major roads in the town.
2. Installation and maintenance cost of sensors is high since there is no Kenyan based company to provide this services
3. The lack of traffic lights that will work in tandem with the receivers, sensors, transmitters and modems to ease up the traffic flow around the town.

In this system it automatically alerts the traffic congestion condition. It can be implemented in the lanes and junctions which carry heavy traffic. Sensors are placed on roads to monitor the traffic condition. In each junction a transmitter and receiver will be present along with a LCD screen for display of message. When congestion is reported an interrupt is sent to the controller and the corresponding alert, LANE BUSY message is sent to the neighboring junctions. The GSM modem (SIM 300) is used for transmitting and receiving messages on GSM network. The alert message is received on the surrounding junctions using GSM modem (SIM 300). This message will be displayed on the respective LCD screen. Thus the rider is alerted for the congestion condition beforehand. This facilitates the rider in taking an alternate congestion free route, avoiding being stuck in the traffic jam (congestion). After the particular lane clears, the LANE CLEAR message is also displayed. This helps in diverting the traffic and hence reducing traffic congestion.

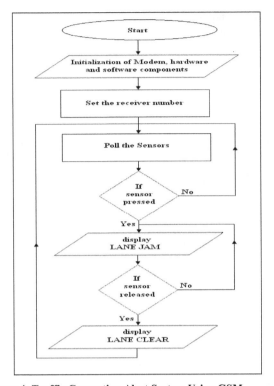

Figure 4: Traffic Congestion Alert System Using GSM

(Jain et al., 2011) clearly presents a simple automated image processing mechanism for detecting the congestion levels in road traffic by processing CCTV camera image feeds. The algorithm is specifically designed for noisy traffic feeds with poor image quality. Based on live CCTV camera feeds from multiple traffic signals in Kenya and Brazil, we show evidence of this congestion collapse behavior lasting long time-periods across multiple locations. To partially alleviate this problem, we present a local de-congestion protocol that coordinates traffic signal behavior within a small area and can locally prevent congestion collapse sustaining time variant traffic bursts. Based on a simulation based analysis on simple network topologies, we show that our local de-congestion protocol can enhance road capacity and prevent congestion collapse in localized settings.

20

(Castro et al., 2010) argues that monitoring, predicting and understanding traffic conditions in a city are an important problem for city planning and environmental monitoring. GPS-equipped taxis can be viewed as pervasive sensors and the large-scale digital traces produced allow us to have a unique view of the underlying dynamics of a city's road network. They proposed a method to construct a model of traffic density based on large scale taxi traces. This model can be used to predict future traffic conditions and estimate effect of emissions on city's air quality. They argued that considering traffic density on its own is insufficient for a deep understanding of the underlying traffic dynamics, and hence propose a novel method for automatically determining the capacity of each road segment. To evaluate their methods on a large scale database of taxi GPS logs and demonstrate their outstanding performance.

(Yuan and Zheng, 2010) proposed constructing a graph whose nodes are landmarks. Landmarks are defined as road segments frequently traversed by taxis. They proposed a method to adaptively split a day into different time segments, based on the variance and entropy of the travel time between landmarks. These results in an estimate of the distribution of the travel times between landmarks. In agreement with macroscopic models, we found hysteresis, coexistent states, and small region of tristability.We simulated the process of obtaining time-averaged traffic data by "virtual detectors". While for identical vehicles, the resulting flow-density data do not look very realistic, micro simulations of heterogeneous(multi-species) traffic offer a natural explanation of the observed wide scattering of congested traffic data (Treiber et al.,2011). Simulation of traffic flow on a road network can also be done by agent based modeling. To define this model, a driver is considered as an autonomous agent whose behavior is based on decisional activities on its environment. The traffic generated is result from the interaction of each agent with the regulations, road infrastructure and other road users

(Wen et al., 2008) used GPS equipped taxis to analyze traffic congestion changes around the Olympics games in Beijing; this is an ex post facto analysis of traffic conditions. (Schafer et al. 2002) used GPS enabled vehicles to obtain real-time traffic information in a number of European cities. By considering congested roads as those where the velocity is below 10km/hr, the authors demonstrate a visualization of traffic conditions around the city can be used to detect congested and blocked road segments.

(Krajzewicz, 2005) explains the use of digital cameras, which are able to observe traffic and gain real information, including the length of jams on a street or trajectories of vehicles. Besides developing these systems themselves, another goal was to invent mechanisms which use such information for traffic optimization. To show the capability of improving traffic flow, he implemented an agent based algorithm for traffic lights control within the microscopic road traffic simulation SUMO.The agent based traffic lights control algorithm is first presented. The main idea was that each traffic light was trying to solve the jams in his front by itself. To achieve this, he looked into the incoming lanes and measures the jam lengths on these lanes. If at one of these lanes the jam gets longer, this lane green for a longer time. Beside these assumptions, several parameters prevented the system from oscillating and from adapting too fast or too strong. This was done by increasing the green phase's duration only if a jam is longer than a threshold. Furthermore, the jam has to occur for a certain amount of time. These are further boundaries for the duration of the phase beside the standard value given at the begin, a phase must not be longer or shorter than predefined thresholds. The whole algorithm shown below is beside the advantage to be very simple, the agent based traffic lights logic can be set on top of existing traffic lights and tries to adapt them to the current traffic amount.

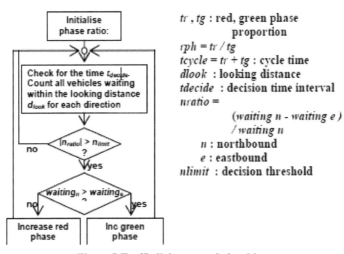

tr , tg : red, green phase proportion
$rph = tr / tg$
$tcycle = tr + tg$: cycle time
$dlook$: looking distance
$tdecide$: decision time interval
$nratio =$
(waiting n - waiting e) / waiting n
n : northbound
e : eastbound
$nlimit$: decision threshold

Figure 5:Traffic lights control algorithm

22

(Balke et al., 2005) proposed a tool that could implement in the freeway management centers that will allow them to use traffic detector information currently being generated in their freeway management systems to make real-time, short-term predictions of when and where incidents and congestion are likely to occur on the freeway network. They further go on to share that the idea is to combine roadway network modeling, traffic flow simulation, statistical regression and prediction methodologies, and archived and real-time traffic sensor information to forecast when and where:

a. Traffic conditions will exist that are likely to produce an incident

b. Platoons of traffic will merge together to create congestion on the freeway.

Krajzewicz et al., 1998) gives an overview over the capabilities of the SUMO software. They look at traffic research being distinguished in three or four classes of models according to the level of detail of the simulation. In macroscopic models traffic flow is the basic entity. Microscopic models simulate the movement of every single vehicle on the street, mostly assuming that the behavior of the vehicle depends on both, the vehicle's physical abilities to move and the drivers controlling behavior. Submicroscopic Models, also sometimes called nanomodels regard single vehicles like microscopic simulations, but submodels are included that describe the engines rotation speed in relation to the vehicles speed of the drivers preferred gear switching actions, for instance. This allows more detailed computations of the emissions produced by the vehicle compared to a simple microscopic simulation. However, submicroscopic models require large computation times. This restrains the size of the networks to be simulated.

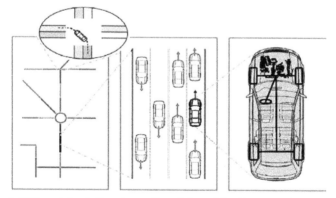

Figure 6: Different simulation classes (from left to right: Macroscopic, Microscopic, sub-microscopic; within the circle:Mesoscopic)

23

A vehicle within a space-continuous simulation has a certain position described by a floating point number. In contrast, space-discrete simulations are a special kind of cellular automata. They use cells and vehicles driving on the simulated streets jumping from one cell to another. In the near future they suggest that SUMO will be extended by other transport modes for buses and such simulations are called multi-modal. Then, the elementary part of the simulation will be individual, who is described by a departure time and the route he/she takes, instead of vehicles as in pure traffic simulations with only one traffic mode.

2.3 Conceptual Model

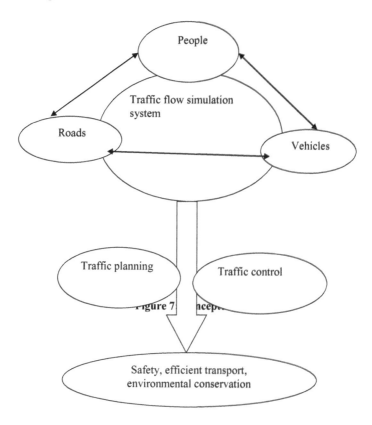

Figure 7   Conceptual

CHAPTER THREE

METHODOLOGY

3.1   Sources of Data and Data Collection

This system will rely on raw data this includes cartographical maps of nakuru county.GPS gadget will be used to gather data of various routes and route names around Nakuru town that are not included in the maps. This data collected will be converted into gtfs format, which will further assist to model public transport traffic flow of the road network. Traffic flow will be simulated by the use of software got from the internet, to try depicting the real situation on the ground. Maps will be used to show exactly where the boundaries are as of where the scope of the study is to reach being Nakuru Town. Other data collection tools namely questionnaires, observation, and interviews will be used to gather information that will be useful to my project.

3.2   System Requirements

The system is required to be able to depict traffic congestion at parts of the road network based on the traffic flow of motorists. Having modeled the traffic flow of public transport around the town, the information will help in marking the bus stops and junctions of the road. GPS gadget will be required for collection of data about the various routes and the public service vehicles plying them, thus easier to simulate traffic flow via software which allows the format of coordinates picked by the GPS device.

3.2.1   LCD display

This will display the simulated traffic flow and the specific points where congestion has been seen.

3.2.2   GPS device

This will be used for collecting data about the various routes and names used by public service vehicles, via coordinates of various points.

3.2.3   Cartographical maps

This will be used to show the existing roads and their boundaries, and also enable to locate the new ones and their boundaries.

3.2.4 MATSim/SUMO software

Data collected by the GPS device using coordinates for longitudes and latitudes will be converted to a different format acceptable by MATSim simulation software. MATSim is a software package for micro-simulation of traffic in urban systems. It has successfully been applied in transport policy analysis, is available on an open-source basis (Balmer et al. 2009). Information about the road network needs to be collected from different government agencies, but in this case will be from map providers. Since the datasets provided are typically not explicitly referenced to each other, they need to be converted to the required format for simulation purposes to be realized.

MATSim couples a time step based queuing simulation of road traffic flow, with a multi-agent travel demand model, based on individual people who carry out daily plans. In our case data is being collected via GPS device. The parameters that will be used include, free speed, flow capacity and storage capacity. The flow capacity limits the number of vehicles which can leave a link in each time step, while the free speed sets a lower bound for the time each car has to spend on a link. Storage capacity is the maximum number of vehicles which a link can contain at any given time. When the link is full, the simulation does not add any more vehicles to a link. The congestion is led to spill back upstream. Storage capacity is calculated from the link length and the number of lanes available.

SUMO is also a simulation package that can be used to achieve the objective of traffic flow simulation. It enables the possibility to simulate how a given traffic demand moves through large road networks. This is an open source tool and a microscopic road traffic simulation package that supports different types of transportation vehicles. Every vehicle has its own route and moves individually through the network. It supports traffic lights and is space continuous and time discrete (default duration of each time step is one second). SUMO has three main modules, that which reads the input information, processes the simulation, gathers results and produces output files. It has an optional graphical interface called SUMO-GUI; NETCONVERT, a tool to simplify the creation of SUMO networks from a list of edges. It reads the input data (from GPS device), computes the input for SUMO and writes the results into various output formats, such as XML, CSV or VISUM-networks. It is also responsible for creating traffic light phases; DUALROUTER, a command line application that, given the departure time, origin and destination, computes the routes through the network itself using the Dijkstra routing algorithm

3.3 Data Analysis

Data will be analyzed based on GPS coordinates got from the various routes. This will in turn be converted to gtfs format so as to be located on the digital map being designed to help in modeling traffic flow. Additionally, analysis will be based on interviews and documentary sources.

CHAPTER FOUR

ANALYSIS AND DESIGN

4.1 Introduction

The main purpose of collecting data for this research is to carry out an assessment which through drawn from pattern, it would assist the road authority policy makers as well as Government or even individuals in making justifiable/sound decisions.

This chapter outlines the analysis and design as well as the interpretations process for the prototype that is to be built for the purpose of this study.

4.2 Description of the Basic Dataset

4.2.1 Data Source

Data to be used for this project is from GPS device which basically picks waypoints, or rather bus stops points as the public vehicle is on transit and halts at specified bus stage. Since the GPS device only picks/collects points in coordinate form (latitude and longitude), a notebook came in handy in recording the various points names so as to later change the ones picked by the former while doing analysis. This data is what the researcher refers to as GTFS data which includes the tracks used by the vehicle to reach its destination and also waypoints, which are the bus stops.

4.2.2 Data Pre-processing

The 147 waypoints had numerous cases which needed to be resolved via cleaning as there were duplicates in some of the points. Renaming of the waypoints had to be done since the GPS gadget only gives the points numbers, and this had to be worked on so as to give them their real names as known by the routes and public service vehicles plying those routes.

4.2.2.1 Data Cleaning

Cleaning of data is basically the next step followed once you have finished collecting data and understood it. The data collected using the GPS device needs to be worked on in terms of renaming the waypoints to their real names as compared to the numbers being given to them by the device. The road map needs also to be cleaned in removing unwanted features that will not be used for instance power lines and also the scope for the map which is Nakuru town.

29

Figure 8: Road Map of Nakuru Town before cleaning

Notice the numbers allocated by the GPS device which needed to be renamed to the real bus stop names. The data collected by the GPS device is in gpx data so it needed to be changed into csv format so that renaming of the bus stops can be realized.

	A	B	C	D	E	F	G	H	I	J	K	L
1	Label	Type	Symbol	Rank	Descriptic	Name on (	Comment	Latitude	Longitude	Elevation	Distance t	Bearing
2	Agape		Flag, Blue	1		27		-0.3031	36.08003	5956.801	0	0
3	Belmax/Jamka		Flag, Blue	2		7		-0.30096	36.07469	5977.7	0	0
4	Bondeni Junction		Flag, Blue	3		4		-0.29761	36.07765	5934.701	0	0
5	Bondeni Police Stati		Flag, Blue	4		33		-0.29645	36.08095	5896.9	0	0
6	Choma		Flag, Blue	5		30		-0.30667	36.07863	5936.299	0	0
7	Deliverance		Flag, Blue	6		43		-0.26821	36.03057	6322.001	0	0
8	Eclipse/Lules		Flag, Blue	7		20		-0.30218	36.07219	5955.499	0	0
9	Eveready		Flag, Blue	8		49		-0.28629	36.04296	6213.199	0	0
10	Heshima		Flag, Blue	9		35		-0.30217	36.08278	5919.701	0	0
11	Kiamunyi		Flag, Blue	10		42		-0.26975	36.03515	6266.099	0	0
12	Kimathi		Flag, Blue	11		28		-0.30481	36.08078	5951.601	0	0
13	Kivu		Flag, Blue	12		26		-0.30214	36.07959	5946.499	0	0
14	Kivumbini		Flag, Blue	13		34		-0.29993	36.08279	5910.6	0	0
15	Langa Mwisho		Flag, Blue	14		11		-0.30494	36.06579	5942.3	0	0
16	London		Flag, Blue	15		40		-0.27721	36.0525	6138.701	0	0
17	Lules Junction/Eclips		Flag, Blue	16		9		-0.30222	36.0719	5974.199	0	0
18	Milimani West		Flag, Blue	17		41		-0.27036	36.0396	6238.1	0	0
19	Mustard Seed		Flag, Blue	18		44		-0.26659	36.02608	6343.701	0	0
20	Mwariki		Flag, Blue	19		18		-0.31585	36.06545	5875.801	0	0
21	NCCK		Flag, Blue	20		25		-0.30045	36.07834	5942.1	0	0

Figure 9: Part of the csv file after converting from gpx format and renaming.

30

Figure 10: Bus stops as viewed on Google Maps.

4.2.2.2 Data Generalization

The next step after plotting the bus stops on the road network and renaming them to their respective names is to convert the file into osm.net.xml from osm.xml. This is done via a tool called NETCONVERT which comes with the SUMO tool. The conversion is so as SUMO can read the file on its platform so as to be able to do the simulation as per the third objective. The road network and the plotting of bus stops were done on the JOSM platform as seen below.

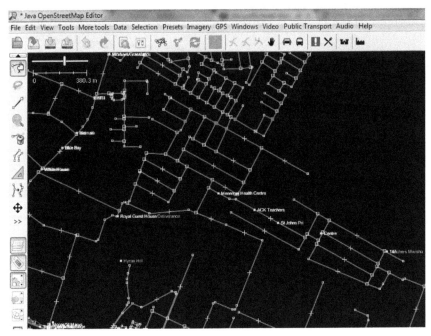

Figure 11: Nakuru town road network and bus stops as analyzed via JOSM.

	Area Covered
1	Town Stage-Pondamali
2	Town Stage-Sewage
3	Town Stage-Langalanga Mwisho
4	Town Stage-Zakayos
6	Town Stage-Lake View/Phase II

7	Town Stage- Kivumbini
8	Town Stage-Zaburi/Kiamunyi
10	Town Stage- Ngata Bridge
11	Town Stage-Gilanis Estate/Soko Mjinga
12	Town Stage-Kenlands
13	Town Stage- Tanners/Weavers
14	Town Stage- Mawanga
15	Town Stage- Works
16	Town Stage-Barnabas
17	Town Stage-Mzee wa Nyama
18	Town Stage- Machine
19	Town Stage- Kiratina
20	Town Stage- Nakuru Teachers

Table 1: Routes Covered

Above are the routes and their respectine route names that were used for data collection of bus stops in Nakuru Town.

4.3 Modelling Tools and Techniques Used

The tools used in the manipulation of data are both open source i.e. JOSM (java open street maps) that is downloadable **from** the World Wide Web used under the GNU license and SUMO for simulation purposes. JOSM was used for plotting bus stops and naming them while SUMO will be used for simulation on the road network.

4.4 Data Analysis and Results

4.4.1 RStudio

This tool is used for the comparison of vehicle counts at the fixed induction loop detectors against the various matatu types.14-seater matatu were the focus of this study but variables were used so as to propose if other matatu types like 25-seater and 33-seater matatus can be implemented on this road network, to reduce congestion

4.4.2.1 Results as from actual data and that simulated by |SUMO given various parameters as got from the ground.

33

Table 2: Vehicle counts and speeds as simulated by SUMO

Time interval	6.10-7.45am	12.30-1.30pm	6.30-7.45pm		Calculated speeds
Stage inbound	129	112	47	(288)	10.81
Stage outbound	53	43	108	(204)	6.73
Town inbound	134	57	35	(226)	8.05
Town outbound	77	83	59	(219)	16.88

	Vehicle counts	Simulated speeds
Stage inbound	294	11.04
Stage outbound	215	7.09
Town inbound	236	8.41
Town outbound	216	16.65

Table 3: Vehicle counts for 14-seater matatus as per Thursday 28/08/2014

Time interval	6.10-7.45am	12.30-1.30	6.30-7.45pm		Calculated speeds
Stage inbound	111	88	76	(275)	10.33
Stage outbound	41	52	116	(209)	6.89
Town inbound	117	62	49	(228)	8.12
Town outbound	69	73	63	(205)	15.80

Table 4: Vehicle counts for 14-seater matatus as per Friday 29/08/2014

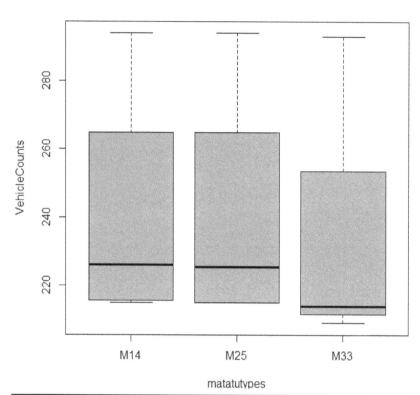

```
>
> sapply(split(data$vehcounts,data$matatutypes),mean)
   M14    M25    M33
240.25 240.00 232.50
> sapply(split(data$vehcounts,data$matatutypes),var)
     M14      M25      M33
1377.583 1394.000 1632.333
> sqrt(sapply(split(data$vehcounts,data$matatutypes),var))
     M14      M25      M33
37.11581 37.33631 40.40215
>
> boxplot(split(vehcounts,data$matatutypes),xlab="matatutypes", ylab="VehicleCo$
>
> fitdata <-lm(vehcounts~matatutypes, data=data)
```

Figure 12: Results from the simulation comparing vehicle counts for various matatu types

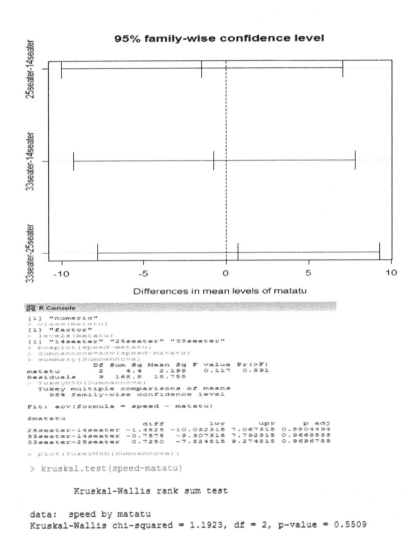

95% family-wise confidence level

Differences in mean levels of matatu

```
R Console
[1] "numeric"
> class(matatu)
[1] "factor"
> levels(matatu)
[1] "14seater" "25seater" "33seater"
> boxplot(speed~matatu)
> Sumoannova=aov(speed~matatu)
> summary(Sumoannova)
            Df Sum Sq Mean Sq F value Pr(>F)
matatu       2    4.4   2.195   0.117  0.891
Residuals    9  168.8  18.755
> TukeyHSD(Sumoannova)
  Tukey multiple comparisons of means
    95% family-wise confidence level

Fit: aov(formula = speed ~ matatu)

$matatu
                   diff       lwr      upr     p adj
25seater-14seater -1.4825 -10.032315 7.067315 0.8804494
33seater-14seater -0.7575  -9.307315 7.792315 0.9669533
33seater-25seater  0.7250  -7.824815 9.274815 0.9696759

> plot(TukeyHSD(Sumoannova))

> kruskal.test(speed~matatu)

        Kruskal-Wallis rank sum test

data:  speed by matatu
Kruskal-Wallis chi-squared = 1.1923, df = 2, p-value = 0.5509
```

Comparing anova test and the kruskal test the p values still makes fail to reject the hypothesis,that was all vehicle speedand counts means are not all the same.

Figure 13:Results from the simulation comparing means of vehicle speeds for various matatu types.

36

4.4.2 SUMO

Simulation of Urban Mobility (SUMO) is an open source, highly portable, microscopic road traffic simulation package designed to handle large road networks. It is licensed under GPL.This tool only reads files with the extension osm.net.xml so conversion had to be done from osm.xml which was realized using JOSM. After the conversion is where SUMO will be used to simulate traffic on the road network.

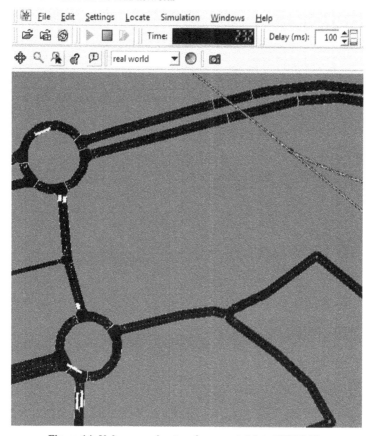

Figure 14: Nakuru road network converted into SUMO file

4.5 System Design

The output of this project will enable the GOK as well as policy makers in the transport industry on making sound decisions. These decisions may include traffic management in the and around the town so as to avoid issues that pertain to congestion that is basically with public service vehicles.

The researcher is proposing a prototype that will assist the Nakuru Town roads and public works department to be able to manage the traffic situation in the town and its environs. Just as private cars have GPS gadgets installed in them so should public service vehicles have them too. The GPS gadgets once installed one will be able to access the road network for the town and his/her location at that point in time and also the traffic situation.

Since the researcher has already pinpointed the bus stops around the town and the various stages in and out of town, the driver will be able to access the town with ease due to all this information is at the comfort of his GPS device. In times of heavy traffic one can access alternate routes to use since he/she can be able to view where he/she is headed and is coming from. This will ease up the traffic menace in the town.

How the System works

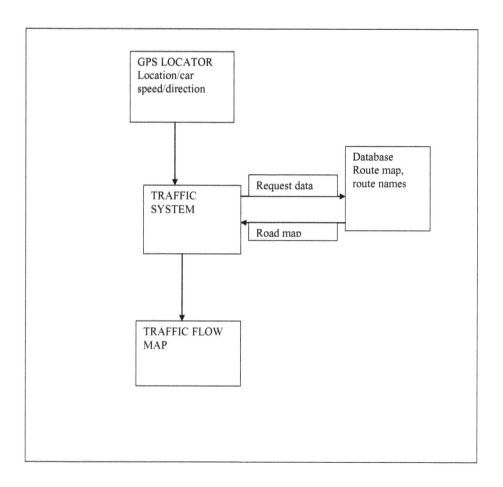

CHAPTER FIVE

CONCLUSION

5.1 Introduction

Simulation is an increasingly used tool so as to mimic how the real thing is supposed to work. In many scenarios simulation has been used to achieve required results and in this case it has been used to achieve traffic management in and around Nakuru Town. The tools used here are JOSM for the designing and analysis of the road network and uploading the bus stops to their specific points on the road network available. SUMO on the other hand has been used to create a scenario that is similar to the real traffic situation on the ground. It has created a scene where vehicles have been allocated to the roads and given destinations as specified with the route names and paints a picture of how the real situation is.

According to the results got from the simulation and comparing it to the actual data, there is a margin of about 10-15%. This goes to show that the simulation given the various variables as got from the ground tends to give a clear view of the situation witnessed on the road network. Viewing the mean and variance from the results got from the simulated speeds and the actual data, 25-seater are preferable as compared to the 33-seater matatus. This can be seen with the way the 25-seater mean and variance tends to lean closer to the 14-seater as compared to the 33-seater matatus. The suggestion here is that not to face out 14-seater completely but by gradually introducing 25-seater matatus. This will in turn increase efficiency in the use of the roads by 25-seater matatus carrying more passengers and easing traffic congestion, while 14-seaters taking care of the urgency bit of the passengers who are in a hurry to reach their destinations.

5.2 Findings of the Research and Contribution to Society

The data was collected first hand was of good quality since the bus stops when uploaded to the road network perfectly fit on their locations even with further proof on Google maps. The research concentrated mainly on public service vehicles since their counterparts mostly have GPS devices installed in them. The research also concentrated on the specific positions where congestion is evident which in this case is the matatu stage being accessed by the 14-seater matatus. Further the general matatu industry around the town was quite interested on how this

40

will impact to the traffic situation in and around the town. In doing the research it was found out that Nairobi has done mapping of matatu routes but has not implemented it on matatus and so it fit they could borrow a leaf from what am doing for Nakuru town.

In line with contribution to society access to amenities will be made easier since traffic will have been managed. With reduced congestion on the roads the pollution issue will be eradicated since the more the vehicles on traffic jams the more pollution is witnessed.

5.3 Limitation of Study

This section will discuss the limitations of the research and challenges faced during the course of the study.

- The data collection process needed approval by the Town office in charge of public works who was on leave and could not give the go ahead. I had to collect data anyway with the help of conductors of matatus I used.

- The system can not be used by any other person until rigorous training is provided to the person to use it.

- It was difficult to collect speeds at the induction detector points and thus vehicle counts were used.

5.4 Recommendation for Future Work

This research did not delve into details of traffic lights which could have coordinated well with the simulation using SUMO software. The traffic lights are currently not working but with liason with the various authorities this would be very helpful in traffic management.

References

1. Massachusetts Institute of Technology. (2013, October 28). Eliminating unexplained traffic jams: New algorithm to alleviate traffic flow instabilities. ScienceDaily. Retrieved February 13, 2014 from www.sciencedaily.com/releases/2013/10/131028141549.html

2. Eliminating unexplained traffic jams - MIT News Office [WWW Document], n.d. URL http://web.mit.edu/newsoffice/2013/algorithm-could-mitigate-freeway-backups-1028.html (accessed 2.14.14).

3. IBM Traffic Congestion - Solutions - South Africa [WWW Document], n.d. URL https://www.ibm.com/smarterplanet/za/en/traffic_congestion/nextsteps/index.html (accessed 2.3.14).

4. Marfia, G., Roccetti, M., & Amoroso, A. (2013). A new traffic congestion prediction model for advanced traveler information and management systems. *Wireless Communications and Mobile Computing*, 13(3), 266-276.

5. Priyadarshana, Y. H. P. P., Perera, K. N. N., Karthik, V., Jayaseelan, R., Abhayawardhana, A. R. K., Sandamali, H. A. K., ... & Weerasinghe, W. R. M. (2013). GPS Assisted Traffic Alerting and Road Congestion Reduction Mechanism. In *Proceedings of Technical Sessions* (Vol. 29, pp. 77-84).

6. Urban Traffic Modelling and Prediction Using Large Scale Taxi GPS Traces - Springer [WWW Document], n.d. URL http://link.springer.com/chapter/10.1007%2F978-3-642-31205-2_4#page-1 (accessed 2.14.14).

7. Jain, V., Sharma, A., & Subramanian, L. (2012, March). Road traffic congestion in the developing world. In *Proceedings of the 2nd ACM Symposium on Computing for Development* (p. 11). ACM.

8. BENHAMZA, K., ELLAGOUNE, S., SERIDI, H., & AKDAG, H. (2013). Agent-based modeling for traffic simulation.

42

9. Aslam, J., Lim, S., & Rus, D. (2012, September). Congestion-aware Traffic Routing System using sensor data. In *Intelligent Transportation Systems (ITSC), 2012 15th International IEEE Conference on* (pp. 1006-1013). IEEE.

10. (Bajpai, 2011) Development of an Interface between Signal Controller and Traffic Simulator.

11. (Pereira, 2011) An Integrated Architecture for Autonomous Vehicles Simulation.

12. Zheng, Y., Yuan, J., Xie, W., Xie, X., & Sun, G. (2010, October). Drive smartly as a taxi driver. In Ubiquitous Intelligence & Computing and 7th International Conference on Autonomic & Trusted Computing (UIC/ATC), 2010 7th International Conference on (pp. 484-486). IEEE.

13. Brydia, R. E., Johnson, J. D., & Balke, K. N. (2005). *An investigation into the evaluation and optimization of the automatic incident detection algorithm used in TxDOT traffic management systems* (No. FHWA/TX-06/0-4770-1). Texas Transportation Institute, Texas A&M University System.

14. (Krajzewicz, 2005) Simulation of modern Traffic Lights Control Systems using the open source Traffic Simulation SUMO.

15. Krajzewicz et al.,(1998) An example of Microscopic Car Models Validation using the open source Traffic Simulation SUMO.